My name is

Let's learn about...

Level 1 - Workbook 2

Focus on sound

Find the objects starting with Harry Hat Man's sound. Then colour the picture.

hat   hand   house

Focus on sound

Draw lines from Harry Hat Man to the things that start with his sound. Circle the one that doesn't.

Draw something that starts with Harry Hat Man's sound.

Stick Harry Hat Man's letter shape here.

Focus on shape

Let's write Harry Hat Man's letter shape.

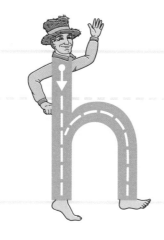 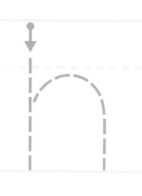 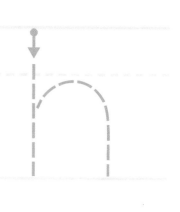

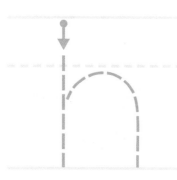 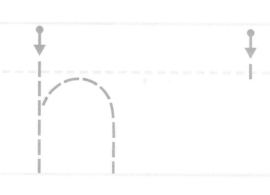

 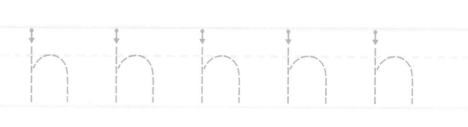

Let's write both his letter shapes.

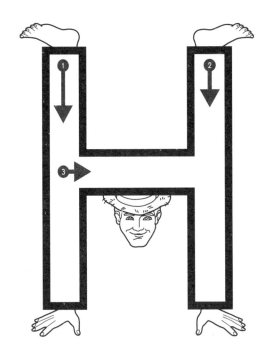

Harry Hat Man

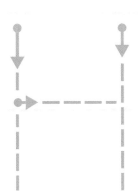

Hh   Hh   Hh   Hh

Focus on sound

Find the objects starting with Bouncy Ben's sound.
Then colour the picture.

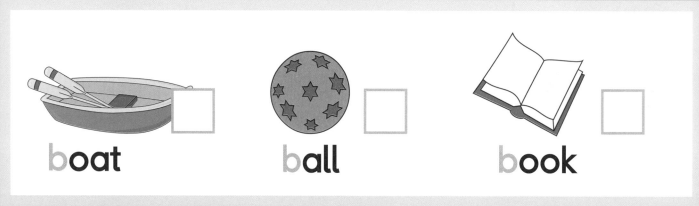

boat

ball

book

Focus on sound

Draw lines from Bouncy Ben to the things that start with his sound. Circle the one that doesn't.

Draw something that starts with Bouncy Ben's sound.

Stick Bouncy Ben's letter shape here.

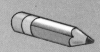

Focus on shape

Let's write Bouncy Ben's letter shape.

 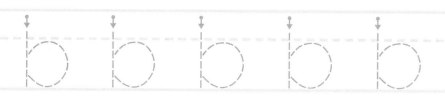

Let's write both his letter shapes.

 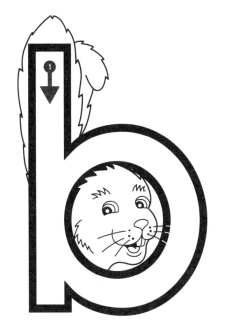

Bouncy Ben

Bb Bb Bb Bb

Focus on sound

Find the objects starting with Firefighter Fred's sound. Then colour the picture.

fish ☐   fire ☐   frog ☐

Focus on sound

Draw lines from Firefighter Fred to the things that start with his sound. Circle the one that doesn't.

Draw something that starts with Firefighter Fred's sound.

Stick Firefighter Fred's letter shape here.

Let's write Firefighter Fred's letter shape.

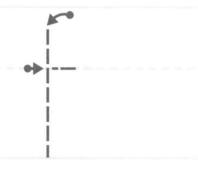

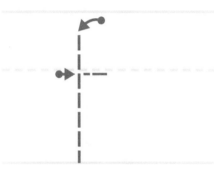

Focus on shape

Let's write both his letter shapes.

Firefighter Fred

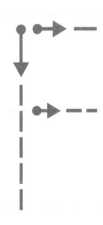

Focus on sound

Find the objects starting with Lucy Lamp Light's sound. Then colour the picture.

log ☐   leg ☐   lion ☐

Focus on sound

Draw lines from Lucy Lamp Light to the things that start with her sound. Circle the one that doesn't.

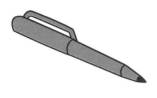

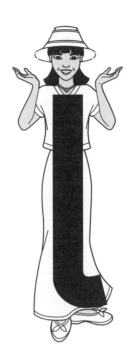

Draw something that starts with Lucy Lamp Light's sound.

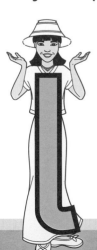

Stick Lucy Lamp Light's letter shape here.

Let's write Lucy Lamp Light's letter shape.

Focus on shape

Let's write both her letter shapes.

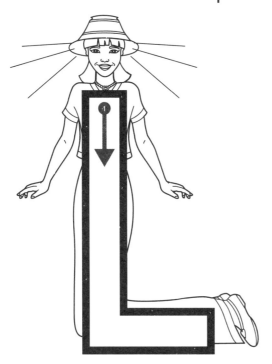

Lucy Lamp Light

Fill in the correct letters to make the words below.

h   b   f   l

__ed

__at

__eg

__rog

Phonic Word Builder

Draw lines to match the words to the pictures.

doll

bed

leg

frog

hat

Now can you write this whole word?

19

h | b | f | l

Listen ➤ Put a tick next to the word you hear. The first one has been done for you.

Track 85

1. ✓ ☐

2. ☐ ☐

3. ☐ ☐

4. ☐ ☐

5. ☐ ☐

6. ☐ ☐

Letter sound Recognising initial letter sounds is an important first step in language and literacy.

Focus on sound

Find the objects starting with Jumping Jim's sound.
Then colour the picture.

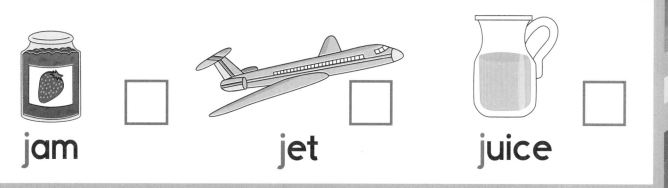

jam   jet   juice

Focus on sound

Draw lines from Jumping Jim to the things that start with his sound. Circle the one that doesn't.

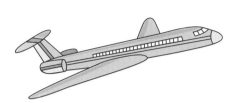

Draw something that starts with Jumping Jim's sound.

Stick Jumping Jim's letter shape here.

Focus on shape

Let's write Jumping Jim's letter shape.

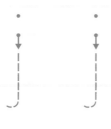

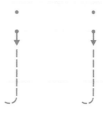

Let's write both his letter shapes.

Jumping Jim

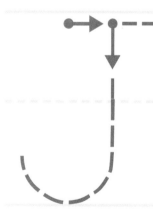

Jj   Jj   Jj   Jj

Focus on sound

Find the objects starting with Vicky Violet's sound. Then colour the picture.

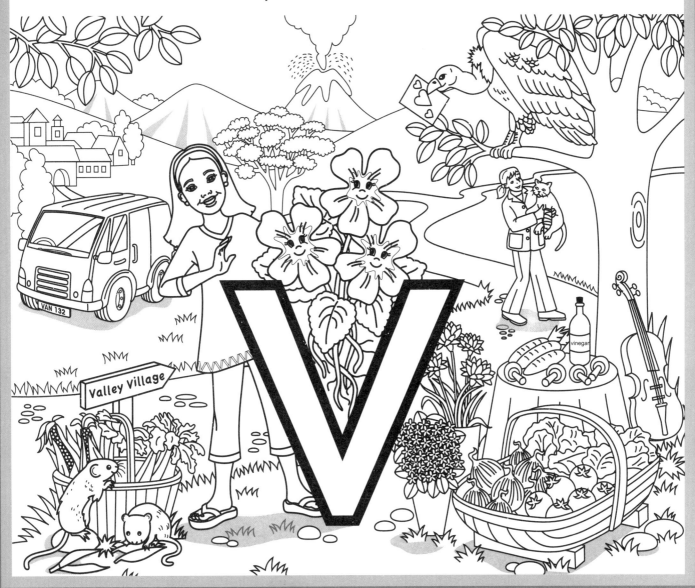

Valley Village

VAN 132

vinegar

vegetables

vet

van

Focus on sound

Draw lines from Vicky Violet to the things that start with her sound. Circle the one that doesn't.

Draw something that starts with Vicky Violet's sound.

Stick Vicky Violet's letter shape here.

26

Focus on shape

Let's write Vicky Violet's letter shape.

Let's write both her letter shapes.

Vicky Violet

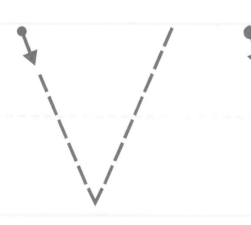

Focus on sound

Find the objects starting with Walter Walrus's sound. Then colour the picture.

water

watch

window

Focus on sound

Draw lines from Walter Walrus to the things that start with his sound. Circle the one that doesn't.

Draw something that starts with Walter Walrus's sound.

Stick Walter Walrus's letter shape here.

30

Focus on shape

Let's write Walter Walrus's letter shape.

 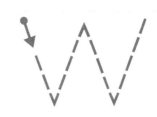 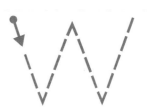

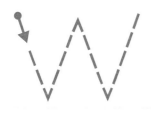 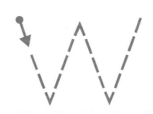

Let's write both his letter shapes.

Walter Walrus

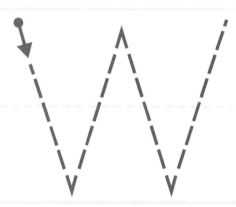

W w W w W w

Focus on sound

Find the objects ending with Fix-it Max's sound.
Then colour the picture.

 **six** ☐

 **box** ☐

 **fox** ☐

Focus on sound

Draw lines from Fix-it Max to the things that end with his sound. Circle the one that doesn't.

Draw something that has an 'x' sound in it.

Stick Fix-it Max's letter shape here.

Focus on shape

Let's write Fix-it Max's letter shape.

Let's write both his letter shapes.

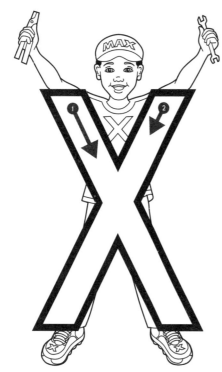

Fix-it Max

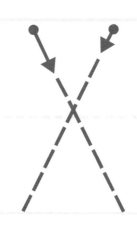

Fill in the correct letters to make the words below.

j v w x

bo _

_ an

_ am

_ eb

Phonic Word Builder

Draw lines to match the words to the pictures.

van

box

jet

jam

web

Now can you write this whole word?

Put the correct Letterland stickers over the plain letter shapes.
Then match them to their objects.

j	v	w	x

Listen

Put a tick next to the word you hear.
The first one has been done for you.

1. ☐   ✓   4. ☐   ☐

2. ☐   ☐   5. ☐   ☐

3. ☐   ☐   6. ☐   ☐

Letter sound Listen to the whole word not just the initial letter sounds.
Be careful, as some words sound very similar!

Find the objects starting with Yellow Yo-yo Man's sound. Then colour the picture.

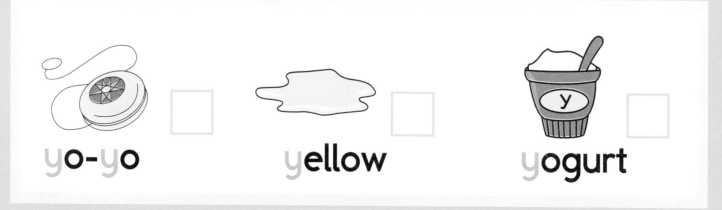

yo-yo   yellow   yogurt

40

Draw lines from Yellow Yo-yo Man to the things that start with his sound. Circle the one that doesn't.

Draw something that starts with Yellow Yo-yo Man's sound.

Stick Yo-yo Man's letter shape here.

Let's write Yellow Yo-yo Man's letter shape.

Let's write both his letter shapes.

Yellow Yo-yo Man

Focus on sound

Find the objects starting with Zig Zag Zebra's sound.
Then colour the picture.

zip   zoo   zero

Letter shapes   Pages 3, 7, 11, 15, 22, 26, 30, 34, 41, 46, 51, 55

h   y   b   ng

v   q   f   l

z   u   x   j

w

Questions Page 87

No   Yes

No   Yes

Review   Pages 20, 39, 60

Vowel Men   Page 75

Focus on sound

Draw lines from Zig Zag Zebra to the things that start with her sound. Circle the one that doesn't.

Draw something that starts with Zig Zag Zebra's sound.

Stick Zig Zag Zebra's letter shape here.

Focus on shape

Let's write Zig Zag Zebra's letter shape.

Let's write both her letter shapes.

Zig Zag Zebra

Sometimes, Zig Zag Zebra's best friend helps her to make words. She is called Zoe Zebra.

Can you find Zig Zag and Zoe hidden in these sentences? The first words have been done for you.

The lemonade is fizzy.

The bee says, buzz.

Whizz! The boy is dizzy.

48

Focus on sound

Find the objects starting with Quarrelsome Queen's sound. Then colour the picture.

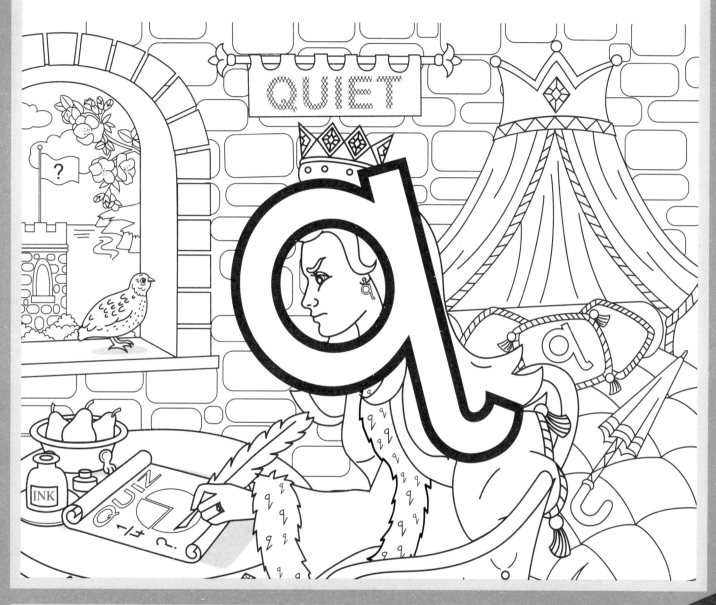

question

quilt

quarter

Draw lines from Quarrelsome Queen to the things that start with her sound. Circle the one that doesn't.

Draw something that starts with Quarrelsome Queen's sound.

Stick Quarrelsome Queen's letter shape here.

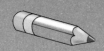

Focus on shape

Let's write Quarrelsome Queen's letter shape.

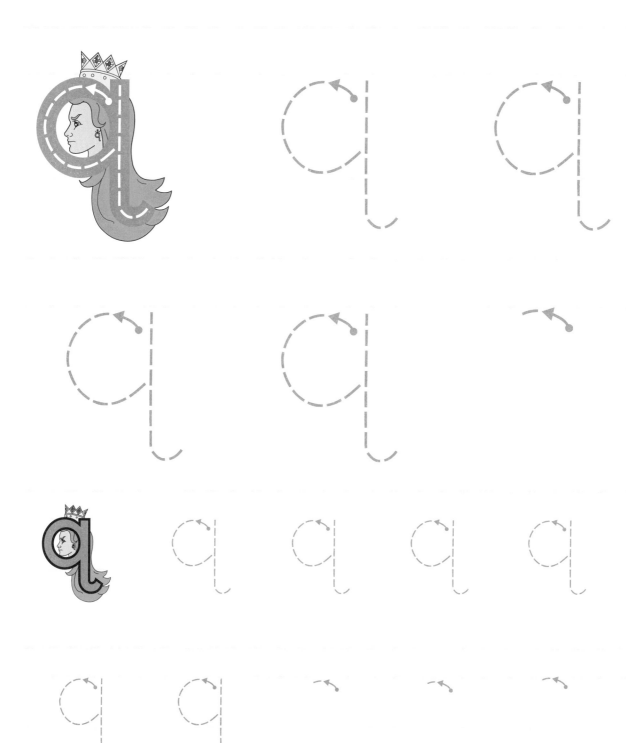

Focus on shape

Let's write both her letter shapes.

Quarrelsome Queen

Qq Qq Qq Qq

Let's review

Fill in the correct letters to make the words below.

y z zz q

fi____

_ip

_uilt

__ak

Draw lines to match the words to the pictures.

zoo

yak

zip

quilt

fizz

 Now can you write this whole word?

c k

Put the correct Letterland stickers over the plain letter shapes.
Then match them to their objects.

y   z   qu

Listen

Put a tick next to the word you hear.
The first one has been done for you.

Track
115

1.  ✔ ☐

2. ❓ ☐   ☐

3. ZOO ☐   ☐

4. ☐   ☐

5. ☐   ZOO ☐

6. ☐   ☐

55

Alphabet Review

Write the first letter in each of these words.

  says 'a...' in ant.

 says 'b...' in bed.

  says 'c...' in cat.

 says 'd...' in dog.

 says 'e...' in egg.

 says 'f...' in five. 5

Listen

Listen to the sound of each Letterland character
and their Alphabet Name in order as you write!

Track 116

 says 'g...' in gate.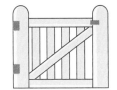

 says 'h...' in hat.

 says 'i...' in ink.

 says 'j...' in jam.

 says 'k...' in king.

 says 'l...' in log.

Write the first letter in each of these words.

 says '**m**...' in  map.

 says '**n**...' in nine.

says '**o**...' in on.

 says '**p**...' in pen.

 says '**q**...' in quilt.

 says '**r**...' in run.

 says '**s**...' in sun.

Write the missing letter in each of these words.

 says '**t**...' in ten. 10

 says '**u**...' in up.

 says '**v**...' in van.

 says '**w**...' in wind.

 says '**x**...' in fox.

 says '**y**...' in yak.

 says '**z**...' in zip.

Focus on sound

Find the objects starting with Noisy Nick and Golden Girl's sound. Then colour the picture.

sing   **ki**ng   **ri**ng

Draw lines from Noisy Nick and Golden Girl to the things that end with their singing sound. Circle the one that doesn't.

Draw something that ends with Noisy Nick and Golden Girl's sound.

Find and stick the 'ng' sticker here.

Focus on shape

Write these **ng** words. Then match them to the pictures.

ng

king

ring

sing

wing

Focus on shape

You will often see Noisy Nick and Golden Girl end**ing** words.
(This is a suffix -**ing**). Let's write the ending on these words below.

waving

jumping

reading

painting

running

Focus on sound

Find Mr A's objects. Then colour the picture.

acorn

alien

apron

64

Focus on sound

Draw lines from Mr A and Annie Apple to the things that start with their sound.

Focus on sound

Find Mr E's objects. Then colour the picture.

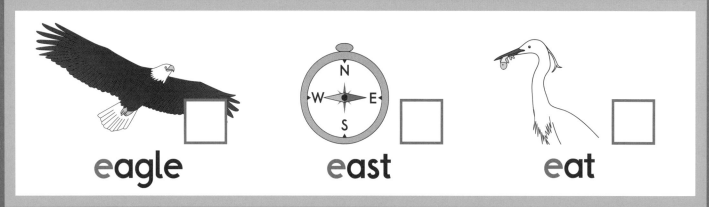

eagle   **east**   **eat**

Focus on sound

Draw lines from Mr E and Eddy Elephant to the things that start with their sound.

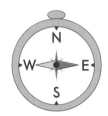

Eddy Elephant

Focus on sound

Find Mr I's objects. Then colour the picture.

Ice cold lollies and fine Ice cream

iron

ice cream

island

Focus on sound

Draw lines from Mr I and Impy Ink to the things that start with their sound.

INDIGO

Focus on sound

Find Mr O's objects. Then colour the picture.

ocean   old   open

Focus on sound

Draw lines from Mr O and Oscar Orange to the things that start with their sound.

Focus on sound

Find Mr U's objects. Then colour the picture.

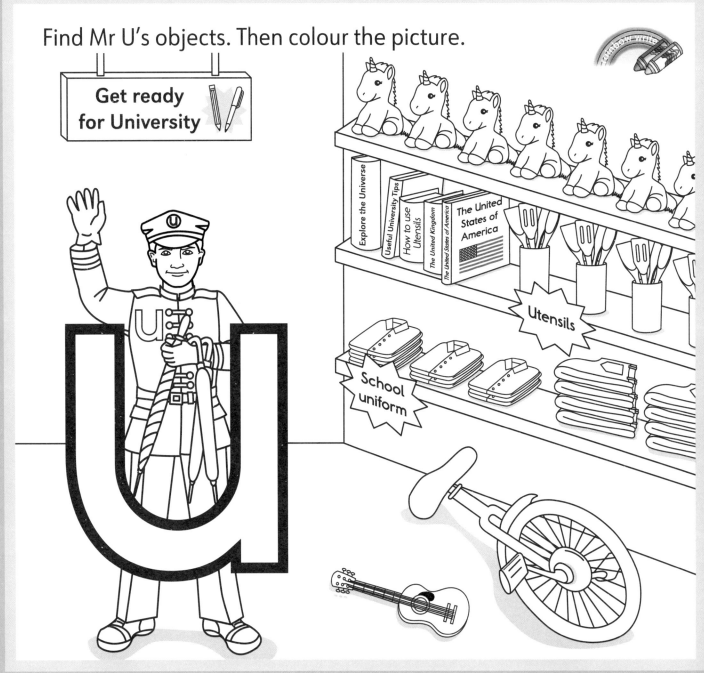

Get ready for University

Explore the Universe

Useful University Tips

How to use Utensils

The United Kingdom

The United States of America

The United States of America

Utensils

School uniform

unicorn

unicycle

uniform

Draw lines from Mr U and Uppy Umbrella to the things that start with their sound.

Vowel Men

Put each Vowel Man sticker next to the Letterlander they look after.

This is Mr A.
He looks after
Annie Apple.

This is Mr E.
He looks after
Eddy Elephant.

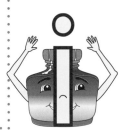

This is Mr I.
He looks after
Impy Ink.

This is Mr U.
He looks after
Uppy Umbrella.

This is Mr O.
He looks after
Oscar Orange.

Letter sound The Vowel Men share the same letter shapes as the short vowels (Annie, Eddy, Impy, Oscar and Uppy).

Look at the pictures. Who can you hear at the **beginning** of each word? Tick the correct box.

 **a**nt ☐  ☐

 **e**at ☐ ☐

 **i**nsect ☐  ☐

 on ☐  ☐

 **u**nicycle ☐  ☐

Starting words

Listen to the words. Who can you hear at the start of the words?

1.

2.

3.

In the middle

Who can you hear in the middle or at the end of these words?

1.

2.

3.

Listen again   Listen again if you need to. The first ones have been done for you.

Focus on sound

Look at these pictures. Who can you hear in the **middle** of each word? Tick the correct box.

 cake ☐  ☐

 jet ☐ ☐

 bike ☐  ☐

 hot ☐ ☐

 cup ☐  ☐

Listen to the words. Can you hear the Vowel Man say his name or the short vowel?

1.  ✔️

2.

3.

4.

5.

Letter sound

Listen again if you need to. The first one has been done for you.

Listen ➡ Listen to the words and circle the Vowel Man whose name you hear.

Track 148

say			I'm		
name			like		
time			make		
no			play		
he			go		
she			use		
me			so		
you			old		
see			be		

Useful words — These are all high frequency words so they are useful to become familiar with. Listen again and repeat the words.

79

Write the correct letter shapes to finish the words.

 _____ own

 _____ ock

 _____ ue

 _____ ag

_____ ack

 _____ ap

 _____ ower

 _____ ame

 _____ end

Write the correct letter shapes to finish the words.

 oves

 ug

 ass

 eep

 ate

 ue

 ide

 ant

 ug

Write the correct letter shapes to finish the words.

 _____ own

 _____ ess

 _____ icks

 _____ uit

 _____ y

 _____ og

 _____ ead

 _____ um

 _____ ab

 _____ iends

 _____ own

 _____ ink

Write the correct letter shapes to finish the words.

 esent

 ee

 ass

 iangle

 apes

 ain

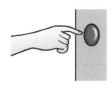 ess

 ice

 een

Write the correct letter shapes to finish the words.

_____ arf

_____ i

_____ irt

_____ ip

_____ hool

_____ amp

_____ oon

_____ op

Write the correct letter shapes to finish the words.

ar

ace

ow

ail

ell

ake

im

Let's review

Write the correct letters on the lines to finish these words.

 ____ap

 ____ag

 ____ant

 ____ug

 ____ick

 ____ab

 ____um

 ____ack

 ____og

 ____een

 ____ess

 ____ee

 ____op

 ____ell

 ____im

Assess · There are assessments in the *Fix-it Phonics Teacher's Guide* to check progress before moving on to Level 2.

Let's read and write!

Can a crab swim?   Add a Yes or No sticker here!

Can a clock skip?   Add a Yes or No sticker here!

A _ _ _ _ sits on a _ _ _ _.

A _ _ _ _ sits on a _ _ _ _.

A _ _ _ _ can _ _ _ _.

A _ _ _ _ _ _ _ _.

Well done!   Now try and write some sentences on your own!

87

Letterland™

Certificate!

This is to certify that

....

has finished

LETTERLAND® Fix-it Phonics Level 1

....

Your Letterland Teacher

....

Date

www.letterland.com